The Day God Pulled My Truck Out Of The Mud

The Day God Pulled My Truck Out Of The Mud

♦

And Other True Stories

Karen Lynn Roberts

iUniverse, Inc.
New York Lincoln Shanghai

The Day God Pulled My Truck Out Of The Mud
And Other True Stories

Copyright © 2007 by Karen Lynn Roberts

All rights reserved. No part of this book may be used or reproduced by any means, graphic, electronic, or mechanical, including photocopying, recording, taping or by any information storage retrieval system without the written permission of the publisher except in the case of brief quotations embodied in critical articles and reviews.

iUniverse books may be ordered through booksellers or by contacting:

iUniverse
2021 Pine Lake Road, Suite 100
Lincoln, NE 68512
www.iuniverse.com
1-800-Authors (1-800-288-4677)

Because of the dynamic nature of the Internet, any Web addresses or links contained in this book may have changed since publication and may no longer be valid.

ISBN: 978-0-595-47182-9 (pbk)
ISBN: 978-0-595-91461-6 (ebk)

Printed in the United States of America

The views expressed in this work are solely those of the author and do not necessarily reflect the views of the publisher, and the publisher hereby disclaims any responsibility for them.

All scripture quotations taken from the New King James Version of the Bible unless otherwise indicated.

This book is affectionately dedicated to the memory of my grandmother, Georgia Brown. You have been gone a long time, yet your spiritual influence upon me is still strong as ever. I thank God for letting you be in my life a short time for it was you who taught me to love him. I will always miss you.

Contents

Acknowledgments .... *xi*
Introduction .... *xiii*
Chapter 1 God Provides Our Needs And Desires 1
Chapter 2 God Commands We Ask 16
Chapter 3 God Commands We Believe 28
Chapter 4 God Commands We Glorify Him 36
Chapter 5 Unanswered Prayers 44

Acknowledgments

A book is almost always the product of the combined ideas, sources, and influences from other people. I want to thank the following people who have helped me shape this book in one way or another:

First and foremost, glory be to God for all things!

Mama, it must have been your love of books that set me on the path to writing from the very beginning. I love you with all my heart and thank you for your unconditional love and support.

My sisters, Wendy and Amy, who have lovingly and patiently lived their entire lives letting me just be me, always off somewhere reading or either hiding away in my own little world writing rather than socializing with them and the rest of the world. I love and admire you both more than you can ever know.

My daughter, Mary Grace and son-in-law, Bradley, maybe now that the book is finished I will cook for you once again and realize that you actually live in the same house as me. I love you.

Bro. Wade Russell, funny isn't it that by helping you years ago with your sermons, I found my true place in this life, that is, writing for God? I will always thank God for you and your undying friendship!

Cindy, Bertha, Glenda, Molly, Kim, and Marcus, my cheerleaders. Thank you for supporting me. I love y'all!

Introduction

A few years ago, my daughter and I were living in the country on an old gravel road. One morning before daylight, I left the house to drive to work. It had rained during the night and so the road was soft and muddy in places. I had not even gotten a mile down the road when one of my tires slipped off into mud and instantly, I knew I was stuck. I pushed on the gas but all that accomplished was spraying mud out everywhere. I put the truck in reverse and tried to back out. Nothing happened. I tried everything I could think of doing but nothing would budge me from the mud.

Discouraged, I faced the fact that my truck was not going anywhere. All I could think about was how I was going to be late for work. My company's work attendance policy was very strict and I knew my job could not afford me to be tardy. I began to feel myself panic. "Lord, what am I going to do? You know I can't be late for work. What if I lose my job? How will I support my daughter and me? How will we eat, or pay the bills?" I felt like crying, and maybe I did for a moment, but then suddenly, I recalled something we had studied in Bible class. I remembered the story about Paul and Silas from ***Acts 16***.

Paul and Silas had been arrested for preaching the gospel of Jesus Christ. They were beaten and thrown into prison with their feet fastened in stocks. What interested me about the story is that Paul and Silas were not discouraged. They didn't ask, "Lord, why did you let this happen to us?"

Instead, ***vs. 25*** says *"But at midnight Paul and Silas were praying and singing hymns to God, and the prisoners were listening to them."*

Rather than being discouraged, Paul and Silas had faith and *showed* that faith through their singing hymns to God. They didn't know how God was going to get them out of this situation but they had faith that somehow, some way he would. Also, by singing hymns to God, they were teaching the other prisoners about having faith. They were glorifying God. So, what did God do?

Vs.26 *"Suddenly there was a great earthquake, so that the foundations of the prison were shaken; and immediately all the doors were opened and everyone's chains were loosed."*

What I had gained from the study of this passage is that with a little faith, God can make something big happen. Paul and Silas were freed from prison, and not only they, but so were the other prisoners as well. The Bible does not say, but I would like to think that having experienced this awesome event, the other prisoners might have believed on Christ also. The scriptures do say, however, that having witnessed all this, the jail keeper believed, was baptized and saved, he and his whole household.

Sitting there that early morning with my truck stuck in the mud, I recalled this story from the Bible and I decided that I was not going to be discouraged but rather, I was going to have a little faith that somehow, God would make something big happen. I decided I would do like Paul and Silas. I began to sing hymns to God. Before I could get one song completely sang, I heard a thundering and the ground shaking. No, it was not an earthquake, but the school bus coming down the road. The driver pulled his bus up beside me and asked if I was stuck. He told me if he didn't have to get his kids to school on time, he could help me. I told him, "That's okay, I understand."

Well, the bus went on down the road to pick up the neighbor's children. Within just a few minutes, a pick up truck came from the same direction the school bus had gone, and pulled up behind me. The driver got out and I recognized him as the father of the children which the bus had gone to pick up. As it turned out, the bus driver had told the children's father about me being stuck in the mud and the father immediately came to my rescue with tow chains and all! He had no trouble pulling me out of the mud and within just minutes, I was on my way to work. And, best of all, I made it to work on time without being tardy!

I was so joyful and thankful over what God had done for me that morning that I told some of my co-workers about it, and this opened the door of opportunity for them to tell me their own experiences about how God had blessed them in the past. If you have ever given a testimony, heard one, or talked with others about true incidents of the amazing ways God works in our personal lives, then you know how uplifting it is, how it can make you feel so good way down deep in your soul like nothing else can. Exchanging God stories with others has a way of cheering you up when you are down, strengthening you when you are weak, giving you hope when the world appears dark, and also has a way of flooding your heart with love. This is why I decided to write this book. I wanted these stories to make others feel this way.

All of my life, I have wanted to write a book, but most of all, I wanted to write a book for God, to honor and glorify him, and I wanted to write something that would encourage faith in others. Getting stuck in the mud that morning turned out to be a blessing because the whole incident gave birth to the making of this book. In the years that followed that morning, I have collected true stories and testimonies from other people about the amazing ways God blessed them and worked in their lives for good. I have tried to include most of these stories in this book along with several of my own personal stories. Some of these stories are awesome and will give you goose bumps just reading them, some are funny, some are ordinary, but all are true, and I have tried to record them to the best of my abilities. Many individuals gave me permission to include their real names and I have done so. Some of these testimonies are from people with whom I have lost contact over the years and I have not been able to seek permission for their real names; therefore, I have created fictitious names for them, but their stories are real.

My truck was stuck in the mud that day. At first, I was discouraged and worried that I would be late for work and that my job would be put on the line, making my whole future appear shaky and uncertain. But, I looked to God, asked for his help, and praised him. There is no doubt in my mind that God heard and rescued me, providing the help I needed to pull my truck out of the mud.

Your vehicle might not be stuck in the mud, but maybe you are stuck in the muddy trials of life. Maybe your finances, family, health, job, or even your love life are sinking deeper into the mud more every day and you just don't know how to get out and back on the road again. It is my fervent hope and prayer that these true stories might cheer you up and encourage you to look to God, ask for his help, praise him and know that somehow, some way he will come and pull you out of the mud. But, whether you are stuck in life's mud or not, I hope you enjoy reading these true stories, and most of all, I hope you experience many of your own blessings from God.

As I gathered information and material for this book, I talked with many different individuals, and through the course of their conversations, many questions and ideas were put forth to me concerning God, prayer, faith and why God doesn't always answer prayers. Having studied the Bible extensively for twenty-four years in both personal and class study, I felt it would be a good idea to include a study guide following each chapter, in the hope that it would give readers the opportunity to share their own personal stories as well as to exercise and grow in knowledge and faith. The study guide is intended for both personal and group study. Either way, it is my sincere hope and prayer that through the study, you will gain as much spiritual enrichment as I have through the writing of it.

1

God Provides Our Needs And Desires

God Provides During A Christmas Layoff

Several years ago when my daughter was in elementary school, I was laid off from my job during the first week of December. I had no idea how I was going to pay the rent, the truck payment, or buy food. On top of all that, I did not know how I was going to ever be able to provide a Christmas for my daughter. The burden of all this lay heavy on my mind and heart. Anxiety and worry threatened to overcome me, but then one day, I decided that I was not going to be anxious! Instead, I made up my mind I was just going to put it all into God's hands. I took all my troubles and worries to God in prayer. I did not know how God would take care of things, but somehow, I just had to believe that he would do it.

Within just a few days after putting my cares into God's hands, some of the members of my church came to visit as they often did, but this time, they brought baskets of food. I had not told them or anyone else about my financial concerns. It was as if someone else had already told them. They visited with me a little while and after they left, I looked at all the goodies inside the basket. To my pleasant surprise, there was money included with the food! Just days following this, a couple of other church members came by to visit and they, too, brought some food and money. Then, just a few days before Christmas, a knock came at my door. When I answered it, there was no one there, but left setting on my door step were several bags of colorfully wrapped Christmas gifts for both me and my daughter. Among the gifts was also a gift card for Wal-Mart. I never knew for certain who delivered these gifts, but I felt sure they were from the church as well. So, through the members of my church, God provided me with food, money I needed for bills, and also a nice Christmas for my daughter.

The amazing part of the whole story is the fact that I had not told one soul about my financial worries, not my family, not friends, not one church member. God was the only one I told my troubles. As one can imagine, I felt relief from my worries and I felt thankful and joyful over the generosity and love of my church members, but most of all, I was completely awed over God's care for my needs.

How many of you reading this are parents? Is there any one of you who does not care about your children's needs and comforts? Most parents would gladly give up their own comforts to make sure their children have what they need. God is our heavenly Father, and as a father, he cares for you just as you care for your children.

Psalm 103:13, *"As a father pities his children, so the Lord pities those who fear him."*
Psalm 34:8-10, *"Oh, taste and see that the Lord is good; blessed is the man who trusts in him! O, fear the Lord, you his saints! There is no want to those who fear him. The young lions lack and suffer hunger; but those who seek the Lord shall not lack any good thing."*

Psalm 145:15, 16, *"The eyes of all look expectantly to you, and you give them their food in due season. You open your hand, and satisfy the desire of every living thing."*

God Is Always On Time

Matthew 6:8 *"For your Father knows the things you have need of before you ask him".*

I have heard it said that "God is always on time". Sometimes, God is there taking care of our problem before we even know we have a problem. My good friend, Cindy Rich, gave me an excellent example of this. Cindy's son, Billy, is in his twenties now, but if you ask Cindy, she will tell you that his being here today is a gift from God.

When she was nine months pregnant with Billy, Cindy went to the doctor one day for her regular check-up. The doctor told her all looked good but she didn't appear to be ready for labor just yet, so Cindy scheduled another visit for the coming week. But, after she left the doctor's office that day, within just hours, Cindy suddenly went into labor and rushed to the hospital.

As soon as Cindy was admitted into the hospital, examined and hooked up to monitors, doctors and nurses began scurrying around her in a flurry of urgency that worried Cindy. Having already one child, Cindy knew something was wrong, but when she asked the medical staff, they all assured her that everything was fine. Cindy was taken to the delivery room almost immediately and as soon as she delivered her baby boy, a nurse took him out of the room right away without allowing Cindy to see him, causing only further concern.

A little later, the baby was finally brought to Cindy and she could see he was indeed a fine healthy baby, but it wasn't until the next day that she learned the reason for all the alarm. The doctor told her "The baby is doing great, especially considering that we almost lost him". Cindy was taken back with shock. "What do you mean by that?" It was then explained to Cindy that when she was first admitted into the hospital, the medical staff could not find the baby's heartbeat and had been worried about losing him. When the baby was being born, he came out blue and with the umbilical cord wrapped around his neck. The nurse had taken the baby away in case he needed immediate medical attention. Having heard all this, Cindy then realized that if she had *not* gone into labor so suddenly that day, her son Billy might very well have been stillborn. Even though Cindy did not understand it at the time, God knew there was a problem before she did and he took care of it.

God Calls In Payment Arrangements For A Telephone Bill

If we are careful to pay attention, we might see that God is often there ahead of us taking care of our problems before we even get there. Several years ago, when I was raising my young daughter by myself and living from paycheck to paycheck, my telephone bill had become overdue one month. It was important that I have a phone and did not want it to be disconnected. I was not going to have the money to pay the bill for yet another week. All I knew to do was to call the phone company and ask them could they please keep it turned on for another week until I could pay it. Before I called the phone company, I said a silent prayer, asking God to please bless me that the phone company would be merciful with me and work with me on this matter. Well, when I finally got a representative on the phone to talk to me about my account, I told her I wanted to wait another week to pay the bill. The representative then asked me, "Well, didn't you call us yesterday about this? We have a note here that says you are going to pay it next week." I was dumbfounded! I couldn't believe what I was hearing! I knew I had not called the day before, and if it was not me who had called, then *who* had called them? I looked toward heaven and said, "God, you are so amazing!"

God Provides A Bed

Another good example of God providing for our needs is how God provided a bed for Heather Prater. Heather is the niece of my friend, Cindy. Heather had been going through some tough times as young people often do and to top it all off, she became pregnant. As the months progressed, the reality became clearer to Heather that she was going to become a mother and that she was going to have another life depending on her. Heather made up her mind that she wanted very much to do good with her life, take care of her own responsibilities, and give her child a good home.

Heather went through the process of getting approved to rent her own apartment, but she did not have any furniture or household goods with which to furnish it. Fortunately, Heather's Aunt Cindy was able to find some needed things at yard sales while other relatives and friends were able to donate several things here and there for Heather's new home.

Yet, one thing still lacked. Heather needed a bed. Her dad, Joe, was able to get some bed slats, but he needed a good, decent mattress to along with them, and no one really had the money to go out and buy a brand new one. Right about this time, Joe, went to the county dump site one day, and when he got there, what does he see? A man was just about to throw out a perfectly good, name brand mattress in almost new condition. Joe asked the man about the mattress and the man explained how his wife was having some health problems and needed a special kind of mattress which was why he was getting rid of this one. So, there was Heather's bed! It is often said that God helps those who help themselves, and Heather is certainly living proof of that.

God Provides His Presence And Comfort In Unlikely Places

II Corinthians 1:3, 4 *"Blessed be the God and Father of our Lord Jesus Christ, the Father of mercies and God of all comfort, who comforts us in all our tribulation, that we may be able to comfort those who are in any trouble, with the comfort with which we ourselves are comforted by God."*

My good friend and co-worker, Bertha Villeges, often wears a special necklace. It is special to her because it is a reminder to her of God's comfort and presence. You see, many years ago, Bertha was going through a divorce and facing many difficulties in her life. The burden on her heart and mind was a heavy one. One day amidst these troubling times, she was having dinner at her parents' house, and for dessert, they were eating a Mexican dish that contains raisins. As she was chewing, Bertha bit down on something hard. She took the object from her mouth and examined it. She discovered that it was a tiny piece of dried stem, probably from the grape vine carried over from the grapes from which came the raisins in the dessert dish. But, for Bertha, this was no ordinary tiny piece of dried grape vine. You see, it was shaped exactly like a cross, and at each end of the cross were tiny knobs, which in all, perfectly formed a shape that resembled the crucified Christ. As Bertha studied the object more closely, she began to feel the presence of God with her. She believed that God was telling her something. God wanted to let her know that he was aware of her troubles, that he was with her, and that he would care for her. Bertha saved the tiny crucifix and placed it inside a small clear bead that she strung onto a neck chain. This experience happened to Bertha many years ago, but she still to this day often wears the necklace as a reminder that God is there when she needs him.

God Shows He Is Listening

Ten years ago, the wife of my good friend, Wade Russell, suddenly became gravely ill. Within just a few days of being admitted to the hospital, her vital signs dropped critically low and the doctor was not sure if she would make it through the night. Wade's preacher, several family members and close friends all gathered with him that night at the hospital and together, they joined in prayer for the health and recovery of Wade's wife. By the following day, her vital signs had made a remarkable improvement, so much that the doctor told Wade, "I don't know how it is happening, but it is happening" Wade then replied to the doctor, "Oh, I know how it is happening all right. It is *God* making it happen."

However, a few days later, Wade's wife did pass away. It was God's will to bring her back home to him, but for Wade and his family during that one night, God showed them that he was indeed listening to their prayers and he did care about their sorrow and he wanted to comfort them. Sometimes God's will is not our will, but if we give him the opportunity, God will give us his presence and his comfort.

God Cares About Our *Desires* And Wants To Provide Them As Well

More than anything else, Hannah wanted a child. She had been married several years yet still remained childless. Hannah longed so much to have a child of her own that in great sorrow, tears and anguish, she went to the house of the Lord and "poured out her soul" to God, asking for a child. God heard her prayer and soon afterward, Hannah conceived and later gave birth to a baby boy whom she named Samuel. Her story is indeed true and you can read about it in the first chapter of ***I Samuel.***

Did Hannah *need* a child? No, of course she didn't need one, but she *desired* a child. It was her dream. We all have desires, we all have dreams. I have heard some people say that we should not bother God with our personal desires. Any one who is a parent knows that when you love your children, you want very much to give them joy. Why do parents ask their children what they want for their birthday, or for Christmas? We love our children and want to give them the things they desire. We want to see them smile, to light up with joy. As our Father, God also wants to give us joy.

Jesus told his disciples in the gospel of ***John 16:24***, *"Until now you have asked nothing my name. Ask, and you will receive, that your joy may be full."*

Why did Jesus say to ask for something? *"That your joy may be full."* God wants us to have joy, therefore, he wants us to ask him for our desires as well as our needs.

Psalm 37:4, 5 *"Delight yourself also in the Lord, and he shall give you the desires of your heart. Commit your way to the Lord, trust also in him, and he shall bring it to pass."*

God Provides A Bigger Bust Size

Here is a humorous but true confession from a co-worker several years ago. Daphni was, well to say the least, abundantly well endowed in the bosom department. One day, several of us girls were sitting around the break table at work talking about girl things when someone playfully teased Daphni about being "so blessed" up top. Daphni then replied, "Oh, you just don't know, but I really have been." And then, to our undivided attention, she told us this true story that I have never forgotten.

You see, until the time Daphni was sixteen, she was fairly flat chested. For her, going to the high school gym dressing room every day was like going to the execution chair. It was torment for her because some of the other girls often made fun of her flat chest to the point that Daphni had become terribly self-conscious about it. The fear of going to the dressing room every day, added with her low self-esteem, drove Daphni to boldly ask God to give her something up top so she wouldn't feel so bad and be the object of sniggering and laughter. It was sometime shortly after this heartfelt prayer, that Daphni's chest did indeed began to grow.... and grow.... and grow. Before she knew it, God had not only answered her prayer, but He gave her *more* than she asked for! You know what they say, "Be careful what you pray for!" Daphni did not *need* a larger breast size and her motive for asking for one was not for vanity, but rather, of deep emotional pain and longing. God showed her that he did indeed care about her feelings and her desires.

God Provides A Publishing Package

My whole life, I have dreamed of being a published writer. In recent years, I have longed deeply to use my passion for writing to publish a book that would both glorify God and also hopefully encourage the faith of others. Over the years, I have let one thing after another hinder me from accomplishing this dream until this past summer when I made up my mind that I was not going to allow anything stop me from finishing it. After doing some research on publishers, I decided I wanted to have my book published with iUniverse, but to do so I needed the money to purchase a publishing package. More than anything else, this is what I wanted to do, so I prayed to God for it. I told God how much I wanted to write and publish this book for him and if he wanted me to do it, then please provide me with the money to purchase the package. Just days after I prayed, the opportunity for an abundance of overtime became available for me at work. I thanked God and took advantage of the overtime and within a month, I had the money to purchase my publishing package. If you are reading this book now, then you know God *did* care about my desires and he surely blessed me with them!

Every one has desires and dreams. I sometimes wonder how often many of these desires and dreams go unfulfilled simply because we do not ask for them.

I John 5:14, 15 "*Now this is the confidence that we have in him, that if we ask anything according to his will, he hears us. And if we know that he hears us, whatever we ask, we know that we have the petitions that we have asked of him.*"

CHAPTER ONE STUDY GUIDE

Part One: Share Your Story

Can you recall a time when you really needed something and God provided it? It could be a physical need such as food or money, it could be protection or comfort. Or, have you ever desired something that was not a need, but God provided it? It does not have to be a miraculous event. God does so many wonderful things for us every day through the ordinary. Use this space to write about it if you wish. If you are studying with a group, you can share your story with others. If this is an individual study, you can write it down to save for future use to remind yourself of God's care for you.

Part Two: Searching The Scriptures

How many verses can you think of or find from the Bible that show God's care for our needs and desires?

Can you find or think of at least one example from the Bible of God providing a need or desire for an individual or group?

Part Three: What About Spiritual Needs?

In this first chapter, I have included true stories about God providing for our physical needs. As we all know, to grow and sustain life on earth, we require physical needs such as water, food, sunlight, exercise, etc. Do we ever stop to consider the health of our spirit? Do we want to grow spiritually, to sustain our souls eternally? Do we consider our *spiritual* needs? I have included the following fill-in-the-blank Bible verses to help us consider some of these needs.

1. **John 4:13, 14**_____answered and said to her, "Whoever drinks of this_____will thirst again, but whoever drinks of the_____that I shall give him will never thirst. But the _____that I shall give him will become in him a fountain of water springing up into _____ _____."

2. **John 6:35** And Jesus said to them, "I am the_____of life. He who comes to me shall never _____, and he who believes in me shall never thirst."

3. **John 3:5** Jesus answered, "Most assuredly, I say to you, unless one is born of_____and the_____, he cannot enter the kingdom of God."

4. **John 8:12** Then Jesus spoke to them again, saying, "I am the_____of the world. He who follows me shall not walk in darkness, but have the_____of life."

5. **I Peter 2:1, 2** "Therefore, laying aside all malice, all deceit, hypocrisy, envy, and all evil speaking, as newborn babes, desire the_____ _____of the_____, that you may_____ thereby."

6. **II Peter 3:18** "But_____in the_____and_____of our Lord and Savior Jesus Christ. To him be the glory both now and forever. Amen."

7. *I Timothy 4:8* "For bodily_____ profits a little, but_____ is profitable for all things, having_____ of the_____ that now is and of that which is to come."

In this earthly life, we need certain things to protect us. We need clothing to protect us from the weather or from the sun. We need shoes to protect our feet from injury. We need shelter to provide for safety and comfort. In the Bible passage of *Ephesians 6:11-18,* God provides us with a list of seven things that we need to protect ourselves spiritually. The scriptures refer to these spiritual needs as "*the whole armor of God*". Can you name these seven spiritual needs?

1.

2.

3.

4.

5.

6.

7.

Memory Verse: ***Philippians 4:19*** "*And my God shall supply all your need according to his riches in glory by Christ Jesus.*"

FOR FURTHER STUDY

Some Bible Passages Regarding God's Care For Our Needs:

Exodus 15:22-27; 23:25
Psalm 121; 55:22; 147:3
Matthew 6:25-34
I Peter 5:7
Hebrews 13:5

Some Examples From Bible Of God Providing For Individuals.

Exodus 15, 16:15
I Kings 17:14-16
II Kings 4

The above scriptures are just some that I chose to include in this study for further reading and research. I do not mean to imply that these are the only scriptures in the Bible relating to this particular subject. I am sure there are other scriptures that one can search and consider.

2

God Commands We Ask

I sometimes wonder how many people realize that it is a *commandment* of God that we ask him for our needs and desires. The chapters of **5**, **6**, and **7** of the gospel of **Matthew** record the sermon that Jesus preached on the mountain. In this sermon, Jesus commands many things, such as: *do not swear; love your enemies; forgive others; do not judge.*

Among these commandments, Jesus states in **Matthew 7:7-11** *"Ask and it will be given to you; seek, and you will find; knock, and it will be opened to you.*

For everyone who asks receives, and he who seeks finds, and to him who knocks it will be opened.

Or what man is there among you who, if his son asks for bread, will give him a stone?

Or if he asks for a fish, will he give him a serpent?

If you then, being evil, know how to give good gifts to your children, how much more will your father who is in heaven give good things to those who ask him!"

Jesus commands this with the same tone he does the many other commandments throughout the sermon. He does not say to ask if you feel like it, or if you want to; he simply and pointedly says to do it! If we choose not to ask God for our needs and desires because we think we are bothering him, we are totally missing the teachings of his word. God says "Ask!"

Remember Hannah from the last chapter? She purposefully and boldly *asked* God for a child. ***I Samuel 1:20*** says *"So it came to pass in the process of time that Hannah conceived and bore a son, and called his name Samuel, saying, 'Because I have asked for him from the Lord'."*

Remember also the popular book, *The Prayer of Jabez* by Bruce Wilkinson? In one simple verse, ***I Chronicles 4:10,*** Jabez asks God for both his needs and desires and *"So God granted him what he requested."*

God Delivers Air Conditions

You should ask my friend and co-worker, Molly Bailey, about the power of asking. This year, Tennessee experienced one of the hottest summers in many years and it was a sweltering hot day when Molly went to visit her daughter and grandchildren at their mobile home. With no shade trees around and no air condition, the inside of the home was unbearably hot. The children were obviously miserable and it grieved Molly that they were having to endure such living conditions. When Molly went back to her home that day, all she could think about was how her grandchildren were so hot while she had the coolness of air conditioning in her own home. Molly knew she had very little money, not enough that would buy a new air condition for her grandchildren. The situation worried and tormented Molly the whole day until she sent up a prayer, saying, "Lord, you gone have to help me with this, show me what to do about this." As the day turned into night, Molly was still worrying over the matter until she had just about decided to take her own air condition out and go put it in her daughter's trailer.

At 9:30 that night, a knock came to the door. Molly went to answer it and there stood a woman who asked, "Do you know anyone who wants to buy an air condition? I got one I want to sell for thirty dollars." In that moment, Molly knew without a doubt that it was the Lord who had answered her prayer. She said to the woman at the door, "Of all the houses you could have went to and you came to mine."

The woman replied, "Well, yeah...."

Molly told her, "The Lord sent you here", and then preceded to tell her how she had asked God for help.

God Drives A Car To Church

And, that is not all. Molly had another story for me about the power of asking. She told me how there had been a time when she had missed a few Sundays of church, but when the next Sunday was about to roll around, she was determined that she was not going to miss church. She got in her car that next Sunday morning and was going to drive to her daughter's house to pick her up also, but along the way, her car began to smoke. Molly said she had not previously been having trouble with her car at all, and for a moment, she thought she needed to turn around and go back home. But then, she thought, "No, this is just the devil trying to keep me from going to church again."

"Devil", she said, "you best just stand on back 'cuz I am going to church and you ain't gonna stop me!"

Molly said she prayed, "Lord, just get me to church." Well, she made it to her daughter's house and told her daughter, "If we can just make it to church, we will find a way home." Well, they made it to church and after the service was over, Molly decided to see how the car would do driving back home. Molly told me that the car never smoked one time the whole way back home!

God Opens A Locked Door

Several years ago, I worked with Tina, who told me she was cooking something on her stove one day and she had to step outside the house just briefly for some reason or another. When she went to go back inside, she realized to her alarm, that the door was locked. She tried and tried to get the door to open, but nothing worked. Knowing that her stove was on with food cooking, she began to panic, and out of fear, she sent up an urgent prayer, "Lord please help me get this door open."

Tina told me, "And the door just opened right up as if someone from the inside had opened it!"

God Heals A Gravely Ill Baby

Bertha Villeges, my sweet friend, told me a very heartwarming story about the power of asking God for mercy and help. Bertha has a daughter named Angelica. Angelica is forty something now, but when she was just a baby, she came down with a high fever. Bertha said she could not get the baby's fever to come down and so she had to take her to the hospital. Soon after examining the baby Angelica and performing some tests, the medical staff scurried in a rush to quarantine the baby. Bertha did not know what was going on and when she asked one of the doctors, she was told that her baby had meningitis. After being admitted into the hospital that same night, the baby slipped into a coma and her health began to decline rapidly. The doctor grievously told Bertha that her baby may not make it but if she did, she would not be normal.

After a few days with no changes, Bertha left the hospital for her home in great sorrow. Along the way, she stopped and prayed to the virgin Mary. She says she told the virgin Mary, "I know that you know how I feel. You are a mother too. I don't want to lose my baby. If you can give me back my baby, I am asking this of you, but

I want her to be able to live a normal life." After her prayer, Bertha went home to rest a little and wash up before returning to the hospital once again. Later when she arrived at the section where her baby daughter was being treated, she was met by one of the medical staff who asked her, "Do you want to feed your baby?" Bertha couldn't believe it! Not only was her baby out of the coma, but she was responsive in every way, completely normal, and ready to be fed by her mother!

God Provides The Rent

Several years ago when I was struggling as a divorced, single mother to work and raise my young daughter, I fell a month behind on my rent. I had no idea where I was going to get five hundred dollars in such a hurry before I was threatened with an eviction notice. I remember my head and heart literally feeling heavy and painful with the burden of worrying about it. I didn't know where else to turn, so I turned to the Lord. I went to God and asked him to provide the money I needed to pay my rent. I didn't know where the money was going to come from. I didn't know how God would do it, but something just told me to trust in him. Something told me to be still and trust that God can provide our needs from sources that we might not even know exist. And, that is exactly what God did!

During this time, I had a friend, Leigh, who lived in the same apartment complex as me. She was in a wheelchair and I often drove her to places she needed to go. I assumed she was just like me, living from week to week. Leigh rolled her wheelchair to my apartment for a visit one day. As she and I were talking, she asked me, "Karen, what is wrong? I can tell that something is bothering you."

Well, I kind of felt bad about telling her, but she asked, so I told her about being behind on my rent. She just looked right at me and so calmly said, "Well, I have the money. I can loan it to you."

All I could do was stare at her. "You mean you have *five hundred dollars* to loan me?"

"Yes, I have some money saved up. I can help you out."

I couldn't believe what I was hearing! I would have never guessed that the Lord would provide through my friend. I had been so down and worried, and all I had to do was ask Leigh! She did loan me the money and I paid her back in monthly installments. The Lord did indeed provide for me as simple as that! It was just a matter of asking the Lord.

God Provides Child Support

My friend, Glenda Robinson, had it worse off than me. Years ago, she too had just gone through a divorce. Unlike me though, Glenda had two small children and a house to keep up but she had not been receiving any child support at all from her ex-husband. Glenda said she had to juggle several jobs just to survive. She told me that she remembered times when she only had five dollars to her name and she had to make a decision of whether to spend it on gas to go to work or food for her and the kids. After going on for some time like this, Glenda finally broke down one day and told the Lord in prayer, "I don't know if I can keep on going like this any more. I don't know what else to do." Glenda says that same night, a knock came to her door. When she opened the door, she was shocked to see her ex-husband standing there with a check for child support.

God Changes A Flat Tire

I will never forget the time when I was in my early twenties and my sister-in-law and I had to go to the grocery store. We had gotten our groceries and were on our way back home through a congested part of the city when one of the car's tires suddenly went flat. We were able to pull off the road safely, but both of us were young and naive and neither of us knew how to change a tire. We were a little nervous with all the traffic zooming by us. One of us said, "Where is a cop when you need one?" We kind of laughed about that, but silently, I did send up a quick prayer that the Lord would indeed send us a cop to help us out. Before I could say "Amen", a police car appeared out of nowhere, whipping around in a u-turn to come toward us. There were two officers in the car and they both got out and changed our tire. They never asked any questions or made any small talk. It was as if they were sent to do a job and that was all they were doing. As soon as they changed the tire, they left. As for me, I was left feeling in total awe that God had just answered my prayer so specifically and so quickly!

If your child needed something or longed for something, how would you feel if he or she never let you know about it? You would feel sad that he or she did not ask you for help, or did not confide in you. Most of us who are parents know that we are willing most of the time to do anything to help our children. We all want our children to ask us for their needs and desires. Is God not the same? Yes, God knows what we have need of before we even ask, but God wants us to think enough of him that we would confide in him, that we would come to him and ask him.

John 15:7 *"If you abide in me, and my words abide in you, you will ask what you desire, and it shall be done for you."*

CHAPTER TWO STUDY GUIDE

Part One: Share Your Story

Do you have a story to share about something you specifically asked and then received of God? Again, if you are in a study group, you can share your story with others. If this is a personal study, you can write it down for future use. It is always a good thing to count your blessings and see what the Lord has done for you!

Part Two: Searching The Scriptures

How many verses can you think of or find from the Bible teaching us to ask or to pray for our needs and desires? If you don't know where to start, look up the words "ask", "pray", "prayer", "beseech", or "request" in a Bible concordance.

Can you think of or find at least one more example from the Bible of someone who asked God for something specific and then received it?

Part Three: What About Spiritual Desires?

In the previous chapter study guide, we discussed spiritual needs. What about spiritual desires? Fill in the blanks of the following scriptures to help consider spiritual desires.

1. *Ephesians 1:3* "Blessed be the God and Father of our Lord Jesus Christ, who has_____ us with_____ _____blessing in the heavenly places in_____."

2. *John 14:2* "In my Father's_____are many_____; if it were not so, I would have told you. I go to_____a_____for you."

Do we really desire heaven? Do we ever ask God to prepare a place for us there? Do we ask God to help us get there?

3. *Proverbs 3:13-18* "_____is the man who finds_____, and the man who gains _____; for her proceeds are better than the profits of_____, and her gain than fine gold. She is more precious than_____, and all the things you may desire cannot compare with her. Length of_____is in her right hand, in her left hand_____and _____. Her ways are ways of pleasantness, and all her paths are peace. She is a _____of_____ to those who take hold of her, and happy are all who retain her."

Do we desire Godly wisdom? Solomon asked for wisdom and received it. Do we ever ask God for wisdom?

Part Four: What About Spiritual Growth?

Do we desire to grow and mature spiritually?

Galatians 5:22 "*But the fruit of the Spirit is love, joy, peace, longsuffering, kindness, goodness, faithfulness, gentleness, self-control.*"

Fruit is something you can actually see as it is maturing like an apple or a peach on a tree. The spiritual traits listed in the above scripture should be things that others can see in us when we walk into a room, when we speak, when we act, and when we deal with trials and temptations. Below, I have made a list of all nine traits of the fruit of the Spirit pointed out in the scripture. From 1 to 9, grade yourself with 1 being your weakest and 9 being your strongest trait. For example, if goodness is your weakest trait, put a 1 beside it and if peace is your strongest trait, put a 10 beside it and so forth.

The purpose of this exercise is to see where you are the strongest and where you are the weakest. Once you decide for yourself which traits are your weakest, go to God in prayer and ask that he might help you to grow stronger in these points. Once you have done this, make goals for yourself to exercise and grow in these traits.

For your benefit, I have listed a few Bible verses beside each trait that relate to this particular word if you want to learn more about what God has to say about it.

____**Love** (*I Corinthians 13; Matthew 5:44; I John 3: 17, 18; I John 4:7-21*)

____**Joy** (*Ecclesiastes 5:18-20; James 1:2-4; Psalm 5:11; Deuteronomy 28:45-47*)

____**Peace** (*Philippians 4:7; Isaiah 26:3; John 14:27; Romans 12:18; Colossians 3:15*)

____**Longsuffering,** or patience (*James 1:3, 4; Colossians 1:9-11; I Timothy 6:11; Luke 21:19*)

____**Kindness** (*Colossians 3:12, 13; Luke 6:30-35; Ephesians 4:31, 32*)

____**Goodness** (*Galatians 6:10; Luke 6:30-35; Titus 3:8; I Peter 3:10-13*)

____**Faith** (*Hebrews 11:6; Matthew 17:20; Mark 11:23*)
Some Bible versions render this as **Faithfulness** (*Rev. 2:10; Luke 16:10-12; Prov. 20:6*)

____**Gentleness** (*Matthew 11:28, 29; II Timothy 2:24; Titus 3:1,2*)

____**Self-control,** also **Temperance** (*Proverbs 16:32; Proverbs 25:28; II Peter 1:5-8*)

Memory Verse: *James 5:16* *"The effective, fervent prayer of a righteous man avails much."*

FOR FURTHER STUDY

Some Bible Passages Relating To The Commandment Of Asking God:

Psalm 50:15
Luke 11:9,10; 18:1
Philippians 4:5,6
I Thessalonians 5:17

Some Examples From The Bible Of Individuals Asking And Receiving From God:

I Chronicles 4:10
Judges 6:36-40; 15:18, 19; 16:28-30
II Kings 6:17

The above scriptures are just some that I chose to include in this study for further reading and research. I do not mean to imply that these are the only scriptures in the Bible relating to this particular subject. I am sure there are other scriptures that one can search and consider.

3

God Commands We Believe

Not only does God command that we *ask* him for our needs and desires, but God also commands that we *believe* he will answer when we do ask.

Hebrews 11:6 *"But without faith it is impossible to please him, for he who comes to God must believe that he is, and that he is a rewarder of those who diligently seek him."*

Notice what the scripture is saying. Not only *must* we believe that God exists, but we *must* believe that he will what? We *must* believe that he will *reward us for seeking him*!

God commands that we ask. God commands that we believe that he will answer.

Matthew 9:27-30, *"When Jesus departed from there, two blind men followed him, crying out and saying, 'Son of David, have mercy on us!'*
And when he had come into the house, the blind men came to him. And Jesus said to them, 'Do you believe that I am able to do this?' They said to him, 'Yes, Lord.'

> *Then he touched their eyes, saying 'According to your faith let it be to you.'*
> *And their eyes were opened."*

Notice how Jesus required for the blind men to first believe before he healed them. When we ask God for something, do we believe that he will answer our prayers? If we don't, we are telling God that we don't think he can do it. We are not trusting him.

I once heard a preacher give the following illustration during his sermon. He said there was a small congregation consisting mostly of farmers and country folk. They had been having a terrible drought all summer and the farmers were worried about their crops, so the congregation decided to have a prayer service to pray for rain. When all the members arrived at the prayer service, only one man came with an umbrella. He was the only one who had faith that God was going to answer the prayer! How many of us are like the man with the umbrella? Or, are we more like the rest of the congregation? We ask, but we don't give much thought to the believing part.

God Delivers A Check

It must have been my God-fearing grandparents who taught me an example of faith early on. My mother told me the story about how when she and her two brothers and sister were small and in grade school, my grandfather had broken his ankle on the job and had to be off of work for some time. My grandmother did not work and one morning after feeding the kids breakfast and sending them off to school, she went to my grandfather and said to him, "I just gave the kids the last of the money for their school lunches." My grandfather told her, "The Lord will provide." Sweet, simple, unquestioning faith. What do you suppose the Lord did? Well, that same afternoon, my grandmother went to check the mailbox and inside was a letter from my grandfather's place of work and it contained money that his co-workers had collected for him. So, my grandfather had been correct in his faith that the Lord would indeed provide. The Lord rewarded his faith.

God Rewards During The Great Depression

I once knew a preacher years ago who told this story about his own grandparents who lived during the Great Depression era. The grandparents had gone to church, and as the collection plate was being passed around, the grandmother noticed that her husband had tossed in all the money they had left. Later, she said to him, "That was all we had left." But, with total faith, the grandfather said, "It is okay, the Lord will provide." Sure enough, soon afterward, the grandmother was going through their closet and when she pulled out an old coat, she found twenty dollars in a pocket, which back then would have been a goodly amount.

God Rewards Edith

My good friend and co-worker, Edith Pearson, knows that God will reward faith. Edith's mother had been sick for several weeks and eventually died. Edith had to miss much work so that she could be by her mother's side. Even though Edith would never have traded those last days with her mother, being out of work so many days did dry up her bank account. A week or so after her mother's death, Edith wanted more than anything just to go to church. She longed for the comfort that it would bring her just being there. But, sadly enough, Edith didn't even have the gas money to go to church. All she had was two dollars. Edith says something told her to buy a lottery ticket. She did and she won twenty-five dollars. Now, she had enough gas money to get her to church and back plus a little extra. Edith went to church and when the collection plate came around, she put in the extra she had left over, keeping *only* what she needed for gas. She could have kept the extra, but she chose to give it back to the Lord, believing it was from him that she had received it in the first place. When she came to work the next day, to her surprise, we had all taken up a collection of money for her.

You see, Edith's motive for buying the lottery ticket was not to gamble. She just wanted to go to church and when she won the money, she only kept what she needed for gas and gave all the rest back to God, knowing all along how much she needed money. God rewarded her faith by providing through her co-workers.

God Rewards For Helping Others

When my father died seven years ago, my co-workers also took up a collection for me. I think there might have been a hundred dollars or so in the envelope. I brought the money home and before I could even take it out of the envelope, a neighbor of mine came knocking at the door. She told me how things had been really hard for her and her electricity had been turned off and she needed forty dollars to turn it back on. Well, all I had was the money from work. If I had not had that, I would not have been able to help her, but since I did have it, I gave it to her. God had always provided for me and I believed that God expected me to do what I could for someone else.

About a week later, I had to take my truck to the shop for a wheel alignment. Inside the shop was another customer waiting on work to be done to his vehicle. The attendant told me that in order to do the alignment, they had to do something else to my truck. I don't remember now what he said it was, but I remember he told me it was going to cost me another forty dollars. I didn't have another forty dollars. I told the attendant to just forget the alignment. Suddenly, the other customer jumped up, interrupting us. He told the attendant, "I need to show you something outside about my car." Well, out they went for a minute and then when the attendant returned, he said to me, "Ma'am, we are going to go ahead and do that alignment for you. That fellow that was just in here offered to pay the extra forty dollars and asked us not to tell you until after he left." I was totally amazed by it all and quite humbled. It was later on that I remembered giving my neighbor forty dollars a week earlier and that is when I realized that God had just given that right back to me! God *does* reward our faith!

Matthew 9:20-22, *"And suddenly, a woman who had a flow of blood for twelve years came from behind and touched the hem of his garment. For she said to herself, 'If only I may touch his garment, I shall be made well.'*
But Jesus turned around, and when he saw her he said, 'Be of good cheer, daughter; your faith has made you well.' And the woman was made well from that hour."

Notice how the woman *believed* she would be healed even before she touched the hem of Jesus's garment.

I Corinthians 2:9, *"But as it is written: Eye has not seen, nor ear heard, nor have entered into the heart of man the things which God has prepared for those who love him."*

Chapter Three Study Guide

Part One: Share Your Story

Have you ever had a difficult thing to ask of God yet you had faith that somehow, some way God would take care of it and he did? Or, have you ever sacrificed something you needed to either help another or to give to God, and then God returned your blessing?

Part Two: Searching The Scriptures

Can you think of or find at least one other example from the Bible of someone whose faith was rewarded?

Consider these fill-in-the-blank verses concerning faith and the reward of faith.

1. **Mark 9:23,** Jesus said unto him, "If you can_____, ____things are possible to him who _____."

2. **Mark 10:27,** But Jesus looked at them and said, "With men it is impossible, but not with God; for with God____things are_____."

3. **Mark 11:24,** *Therefore I say to you, whatever things you____when you pray, _____that you receive them, and you_____have them.*

4. **Luke 6:38,** *_____, and it will be_____to you: good measure, pressed down, shaken together, and running over will be put into your bosom. For with the same_____that you use, it will be measured_____to you.*

5. **James 2:26,** *For as the body without the spirit is dead, so_____without_____is dead also.*

Part Three: Exercising Your Faith

If you read **Hebrews 11,** you will read a list of people who all lived throughout the generations of the Bible, people who lived by faith in God and who received blessings because of their faith. This passage in the Bible is sometimes referred to as the "Hall of Faith". What is really great about this is that after two thousand years, these people are still remembered and recorded in the Bible for their faith. Wouldn't it be great to have your name recorded in the Hall of Faith? If your name was going to be added to this list, what would it say about your faith? What would you like future generations to remember you by? Write your own entry for the Hall of Faith as you would like your faith to be remembered.

Memory Verse: Hebrews 11:6 *"But without faith it is impossible to please him, for he who comes to God must believe that he is, and that he is a rewarder of those who diligently seek him."*

FOR FURTHER STUDY

Some Bible Individuals Who Were Rewarded For Their Faith:

Hebrews 11:7, 8
Joshua 2:1-21; 6:21-25
Daniel 3
I Samuel 17
Luke 2:25-32; 2:36-38

The above scriptures are just some that I chose to include in this study for further reading and research. I do not mean to imply that these are the only scriptures in the Bible relating to this particular subject. I am sure there are other scriptures that one can search and consider.

4

God Commands We Glorify Him

I once heard it said that telling others what God has done for you is bragging, and we should not do it. However, God commands that we glorify him, that we tell others what he has done for us. It is not ourselves that we are bragging about, but rather it is *God* that we are bragging about!

Matthew 5:16 *"Let your light so shine before men, that they may see your good works and glorify your Father in heaven."*

Psalm 50:15, *"Call upon me in the day of trouble; I will deliver you, and you shall glorify me."*

After Jesus healed a man possessed with a demon, Jesus told him in **Mark 5:19**, *"Go home to your friends, and tell them what great things the Lord has done for you, and how he has had compassion on you."*

Why glorify God? Why should we tell others the great things God has done for us? Because, it encourages others to want to come to him, believe in him, and trust in him.

In the gospel of *John 4*, Jesus met a Samaritan woman at a well and had a conversation with her in which he taught her about true worship and how he was the living water and anyone who came to him would never thirst again. When the woman told Jesus that she had no husband, Jesus told her she was speaking the truth because she had previously had five husbands and the man she presently lived with was not her husband. When Jesus told her this, she was awed that he could know these things about her having never before met her, and she realized he must surely be a prophet.

Jesus plainly taught her that he was indeed the Messiah, the Christ, and she believed him. After this, she went into the city and told others there about the man she had met at the well. She told them to come and see him for themselves. Many of them went to see this man at the well that she had told them about and *vs. 39* says, *"And many of the Samaritans of that city believed in him because of the word of the woman who testified, 'He told me all that I ever did.'"*

Notice that *many* Samaritans believed in Jesus because the woman had told them about him. What if she had kept everything to herself and never told anyone? *Many* still would have been lost without Jesus.

Almost Persuaded

Years ago, I worked with a man named Tom, who admitted that he just simply did not believe in God. He believed that Jesus was a man who once lived and taught many good things, but he did not believe that Jesus performed any miracles. Tom was a good, friendly person and he loved a good debate. He knew how I felt about God and the Bible, so he often would engage me in a friendly debate over the Bible. We did this off and on over the period of a few years. Then, one day, he was feeling really discouraged and told me some problems he was having in his life. Of course, I just felt like I had to tell him what I always did when I was troubled. I went to God in prayer. Tom listened to me as I talked. This time, he didn't try to debate me. He just listened. I began to tell him about times that I had asked God for help and how God had never let me down. I told him some of the wonderful things God had done for me. As I told these things to Tom, he just listened, and after a while, he said so sincerely to me, "Karen, you make me *want* to believe."

This is why God wants us to tell others the great things he does for us. Not everyone believes in God and God wants all to come to him. Then, some people do believe in God, but their faith is not very strong and they need encouraging.

Telling Others How God Provided Me With A Brand New Truck

Ten years ago, I had just gone through my divorce and I was raising my daughter on my own. I needed dependable transportation to make sure I got back and forth to work every day because I could not afford to lose my job over a car that might be breaking down every time I turned around. So, I went to a local dealership and looked at a new pick up truck. I did not know if I could be approved for a loan on the truck or not. Just before the divorce, my husband and I had filed bankruptcy and aside from that, I had never before had any credit established in my own name. I wanted the truck very much. I wanted to have the confidence of a dependable vehicle since I was out on my own. Before I returned to the dealership to check on my approval, I prayed to God about it. I told God why I wanted the truck, and I promised him that if he would bless me with it, I would tell others how he had answered my prayer and blessed me with it. I wanted to glorify him with it.

Well, that has been ten years now, and guess what? I am still driving that truck! It has almost four hundred thousand miles on it!

A few months ago, the timing belt went out on it. That was the first major work I had ever had done to it in ten years, outside of normal wear and tear. The mechanic who repaired the timing belt asked me, "Have you ever had a timing belt change before on this truck?"

I said, "No."

He was shocked. "You mean to tell me that this one timing belt has lasted for almost four hundred thousand miles? That's pretty amazing. Most timing belts are only good for one hundred thousand."

I just smiled and told him that God had blessed me all these years with that truck.

Ten years ago, I asked God for a new truck and I promised to tell others how he had blessed me with it. At first, I only told a few people, but as time went on and my truck proved to be dependable, never letting me down, the more I told others how God had blessed me with it. As the truck now has aged and the mileage increased, still with no troubles, more and more people are surprised with it and often ask me about it. I always tell them. "I have been very blessed by God with it." Often, I will tell them the whole story.

There is not a day that goes by that I don't thank God for my truck. There is no doubt in my mind that the reason it has run all these years so dependably is because of the hand of God. I will continue to tell others how much God has blessed me with it because I promised God all those years ago that I would glorify him. God answered my prayer in giving me the truck. I have tried to keep my promise to tell others about it, and God has continued to heap blessing after blessing on top of it all these years!

I Corinthians 6:20 *"For you were bought at a price; therefore glorify God in your body and in your spirit, which are God's."*

CHAPTER FOUR STUDY GUIDE

Part One: Share Your Story

Have you ever praised or glorified God a little and he made something big happen? If you can't think of something to write here, then go back to Chapters One, Two, and Three. Did you have a story to tell about how God has blessed you? If so, then use it to glorify God now. Tell someone about how God has blessed you. Watch and see how this can uplift and cheer someone, or encourage their faith in God.

Part Two: Searching The Scriptures

How many scriptures from the Bible can you think of or find which give an example to glorify or praise God?

Can you answer the following trivia questions concerning two individuals in the Bible who were guilty of *not* giving glory to God?

1. *I was a king who gave a speech to the people of Tyre and Sidon and when they heard me speak, they shouted, "The voice of a god and not of a man!" I accepted their praise and did not give the glory to God. Then immediately, an angel of the Lord struck me so that I was eaten by worms and I died.*

Who am I?

2. *I was the ruler of the great Babylonian empire. I believed that I had built Babylon with my own might and power, but God taught me a lesson by stripping me of my kingdom and making me to be no better than the animals. God caused me to eat grass like the oxen. My hair grew like the feathers of the eagle and my nails grew like the claws of a bird. After all this, I learned understanding that it was the most High God who had given me my kingdom and not my own might and power. When I understood this, I praised and honored God, and he then returned my kingdom to me plus even added more to it.*

Who am I?

Part Three: Exercising Your Faith

Read ***Exodus 33:1-23.*** By God's instructions, Moses and the children of Israel were to begin their journey to the promised land. Moses did not want to go the journey without God. He wanted the presence of God to be with him as they journeyed to the promised land. Moses wanted reassurance from God, so Moses asked God simply, *"Please show me your glory."*

Have you ever seen the glory of God? Ever seen a glimpse of God? If God has ever answered your prayer, rewarded your faith, made something good happen to you, then you have seen a glimpse of God's glory.

From time to time, our faith may grow weak and we need reassurance. During these times, we should be like Moses and simply ask God, "Please show me your glory." Ask God for his presence, for just a glimpse of his glory, and watch what God will do.

When Moses came down from the mountain after seeing the glory of God, talking with and receiving the ten commandments from God, the Bible says that the face of Moses shined so brightly that it was difficult for the people to look at him. In this sense, Moses was literally reflecting the light of God to the people. Seeing the glory of God caused Moses to shine with God's light and it reflected to those around him.

When God shines his glory to us by answering a prayer, providing for us, comforting us, or working in our lives for good, we are often filled up with love and joy. But, do we hide that joy, or do we reflect it to those around us? When the people saw the face of Moses, there was no doubt for them that he had seen God. When people see our faces, can they tell if God is with us? Do we shine his joy and love?

I Peter 3:15 "But sanctify the Lord God in your hearts, and always be ready to give a defense to everyone who asks you a reason for the hope that is in you, with meekness and fear."

Do we ever give others a reason to wonder why we are always happy, peaceful, confident even in bad times as well as good? We can glorify God just by letting others see the happiness that he gives us.

Memory Verse: *I Corinthians 10:31* *"Therefore, whether you eat or drink, or whatever you do, do all to the glory of God."*

FOR FURTHER STUDY

Some Bible Passages Regarding Glorifying God:

Psalm 22:23; 50:15; 103:1
Matthew 9:8
Luke 13:13; 17:15
Acts 4:21
Romans 15:6
I Peter 2:12; 4:11; 4:14, 16

Answers to Trivia Questions

1. Acts 12:20-23

2. Daniel 4

The above scriptures are just some that I chose to include in this study for further reading and research. I do not mean to imply that these are the only scriptures in the Bible relating to this particular subject. I am sure there are many other scriptures that one can search and consider.

5

Unanswered Prayers

"Well, I believe in God, but he doesn't answer my prayers." I have heard this from a few people. One person in particular even told me that in his forty-two years of life, God had never once answered one solitary prayer for him.

Why do some people *not* get answered prayers from God? Well, no one can answer that question with certainty, but I do have some Biblically grounded thoughts to offer for consideration.

God Knows What Is Up The Road

Sometimes our unanswered prayers are blessings in and of them themselves. God knows our needs. He knows what is best for us, and he knows what lies in the future when we don't. Sometimes, God doesn't answer a prayer because he has something better planned for us than what we have asked of him.

I had worked for the same company for sixteen years. I loved my job, and my co-workers were like family to me. When rumors spread around that the company may close its doors down, I panicked. I did not want that to happen. I began to pray to God that He would cause good things to happen so that our company would not shut down. I prayed for this often and for many days and weeks.

But, alas, the company did shut down and my job came to an end. God did not answer that prayer.

But, guess what? Soon after, God provided me with a new job much closer to home, a job that paid more, a job that I actually enjoyed doing, a job that gave me more opportunity for overtime, good benefits and a whole new great work family of good, friendly people! As much as I enjoyed working for the first company, I can now look back and see that God blessed me by *not* answering my prayer! If God *had* answered my prayer, I would still be driving a further distance to work with higher gas prices, not making as much money, and not as much opportunity for overtime. By not answering my prayer, God gave me much greater blessings!

God Says No To Keep A Job

My mother has a similar experience. She had worked with the same company for many years but was not happy with that job. She learned that another local company was hiring. This other company offered much greater wages and benefits so she turned in her application. She wanted this job so much that she began to pray that she would get hired on and she asked others to pray for her as well. But, my mother did not get hired. God did not answer her prayer. A few months passed and we learned that this other company was laying off many people. It was then we realized that had my mother been hired on, she would now be out of a job. God knew what was up the road and by *not* answering her prayer, he was blessing her! She still works at the same place, but at least she has a steady job, seniority, and status.

Sometimes, God Wants Us To Exercise Our Faith.

We have already covered how God commands that we ask and that we believe he will answer. We must have faith to please God and we must believe that he will reward that faith. God does not reward doubtfulness. He rewards faith!

In **Mark 9:14-29**, a father brought his epileptic child to the disciples of Christ to ask them to heal him, but try as they might, the disciples could not heal him. So, when the father saw Jesus coming, he took the child to Jesus.

Notice what the father says to Jesus. *"But **if** you can do anything, have compassion on us and help us."* The father was not strong in his faith. He obviously doubted because he tells Jesus, *"**If** you can do anything."*

Now watch how Jesus replies to the father. *"**If** you can believe, all things are possible to him that believes."* You see, Jesus was pointing out the father's doubtfulness and wanted to encourage the man to believe.

The father understands then that it is his weak faith which is holding his blessings back, because with tears, he cries to Jesus, *"Lord, I believe; help my **unbelief**!"*

Jesus then healed the man's son of the epileptic spirit. Afterward, Jesus's disciples asked him why were they unable to heal the child. Jesus answered, *"This kind can come out by nothing but prayer and fasting."*

You see, just like Jesus knew that the father's faith was weak and needed strengthening, so God knows when our faith is weak. Sometimes, God wants us to do more than just ask for something. He wants us to *show* a little faith, to exercise that faith. Maybe we need to fast, maybe we need to get out our Bibles and study to strengthen our faith. Maybe we need to examine ourselves for any sin in our life that we need to repent of and make our hearts right with God. Sometimes, there is something amiss in our lives that is making us weak in faith and God wants us to exercise that faith to make it stronger. We know that our bodies will grow weak without exercise and so will our souls grow weak without exercise!

Sometimes We Are Just Blind And Unthankful

Maybe sometimes we don't get answered prayers because we are not willing to open our eyes and see just how much God *does* bless us! Thankfulness and faith go hand in hand. Do we recognize the blessings that God gives us every day? Do we see that God blesses us with our health, shelter, clothes, transportation, jobs, food? Every day that we wake up, do we see that it is another blessing from God? Every time we get in our vehicles and drive safely to our destinations, do we see that God protected us? Every time something comes up to cause us concern and then we see it all get worked out satisfactorily, do we see that it is God who took care of it? Do we see these little blessings that come and go every single day of our lives? And, do we ever stop to thank him for these blessings? If we never acknowledge God, why should he acknowledge us?

James 4:8 "*Draw near to God and he will draw near to you.*"

2 Chronicles 15:2 "*The Lord is with you while you are with him. If you seek him, he will be found by you; but if you forsake him, he will forsake you.*"

Thankfulness And Faith Go Hand In Hand

Luke 17:12-19 "*Then as he entered a certain village, there met him ten men who were lepers, who stood afar off.*

> *And they lifted up their voices and said, 'Jesus, Master, have mercy on us!'*
> *So when he saw them, he said to them, 'Go, show yourselves to the priests.' And so it was that as they went, they were cleansed.*
> *And one of them, when he saw that he was healed, returned, and with a loud voice glorified God, and fell down on his face at his feet, giving him thanks. And he was a Samaritan.*
> *So Jesus answered and said, 'Were there not ten cleansed? But where are the nine? Were there not any found who returned to give glory to God except this foreigner?*
> *And he said to him, 'Arise, go your way. Your faith has made you well.'"*

Why did Jesus tell the leper his faith had made him well? Because he *showed* his faith. He exercised it. He was the only one out of ten that acknowledged what God had done for him and he was the only one who made an effort to give thanks.

If it seems like God is not answering our prayers, maybe it is because we are not grateful for the many things he already does for us.

My friend, Glenda Robinson, says it well. She says "If I can see or talk to my mother, my sisters, and my children every day and then go to sleep beside my husband every night in our own bed rather than a hospital bed, it can't get any better than that and I am so thankful to God, and I tell him so."

Is There Something Hindering My Prayers?

I Peter 3:7 *"Husbands, likewise dwell with them with understanding, giving honor to the wife, as to the weaker vessel, and as being heirs together of the grace of life, that your prayers may be not hindered."*

The apostle Peter is instructing husbands to treat their wives with honor and respect here. Why? Because he says that both husbands and wives are *heirs together in the grace of life*. If they are not in a right relationship with each other, how can they be in a right relationship with God? Think about it. If you are angry or resentful at your spouse, it is not always easy to be humble and to pray to God with the right attitude.

But, this doesn't just apply to husbands and wives. It can also apply to our relationships with anyone. If we are having a bad relationship with someone, it can hinder us from being right with God.

Matthew 5:23, 24 *"Therefore if you bring your gift to the altar, and there remember that your brother has something against you, leave your gift there before the altar, and go your way. First be reconciled to your brother, and then come and offer your gift."*

You see, as God's children, our heavenly father desires that we all love and respect one another. God does not want us coming to him in prayer while all along we know we have either done something wrong to another or we are holding a grudge in our hearts toward someone else. When we are harboring a grudge toward someone, it casts a dark shadow around our hearts. This dark shadow stands between us and God. When we come to God in prayer, God wants our hearts to be pure, to be free of hate, to be free of grudges, free of negativity. And, certainly, if we have done something wrong to someone else, God expects us to make it right with that person or else we can not be right with God. These things can hinder our prayers from being heard or answered by God.

I John 4:7,8, 20 *"Beloved, let us love one another, for love is of God; and everyone who loves is born of God and knows God. He who does not love does not know God, for God is love."*

"If someone says, 'I love God,' and hates his brother, he is a liar; for he who does not love his brother whom he has seen, how can he love God whom he has not seen?"

Is My Relationship With God A One-way Street Or A Two-way Street?

John 9:31 *"Now we know that God does not hear sinners; but if anyone is a worshiper of God and does his will, he hears him."*

How can God answer our prayers if he does not even hear them? But notice, whom does God hear? Those that are worshipers of God and those that do his will.

If we don't seem to be getting any response from God, maybe it is time we should ask ourselves what kind of relationship do we have with God? Is it a one-way street? Do we only acknowledge God when we need him?

Having a relationship with God is just like having a relationship with our spouse, child, friend or anyone else. Suppose you had a loved one who called you or came around only when they wanted something, but when you needed something from them, they were never there for you? You would not like that very much. Chances are, after enough of that kind of treatment, you would probably ignore them when they do call. God does not want to be treated that way either. We want the people we love to listen to us when we talk to them. We want them to come visit us, to share things with us, to do things with us, support us in our goals. And, we want them to avoid doing the things that hurt our feelings and disappoint us. We want them to be faithful and loyal to us.

God is the same with us. He loves us and wants us to listen to him. He wants us to read his word, hear what he has to say to us. He wants us visit him in prayer and in worship. He wants us to support him, to shine his light to the world. And, he wants us to be loyal and faithful to him, to avoid the things that disappoint him.

John 15:7 *"If you abide in me, and my words abide in you, you will ask what you desire, and it shall be done for you."*

Notice, Jesus wants a two-way relationship here with us! You abide in me and I abide in you. It has to work both ways!

I John 3:22 *"And whatever we ask we receive from him, because we keep his commandments and do those things that are pleasing in his sight."*

Why do we receive the things we ask of God? Because we "keep his commandments and do those things pleasing in his sight."

Is There Something Standing Between Me And God?

Isaiah 59:1 *"Behold, the Lord's hand is not shortened, that it cannot save; nor his ear heavy, that it cannot hear.*
But your iniquities have separated you from your God; and your sins have hidden his face from you, so that he will not hear."

Ever notice how dogs knows when they have done something wrong, like when they have chewed up the toilet paper? They will often run and hide under something. They know they are guilty and they are ashamed and they allow this guilt to separate them from their loving owners. On the other hand, many cats also know when they have done wrong, like tearing the toilet paper in shreds throughout the house. They, too, often will run and hide from their owners, but they do it in a rebellious manner, striking their tails back and forth in stubbornness.

Either way, the ashamed dog or the rebellious cat both allow their wrongdoing to keep them from the loving hand of their owners. How can you pet and play with a dog that won't come out of his hiding place? And, a rebellious cat will not allow you to come near it until it finally decides to surrender to you.

You see, people are the same with God. Some live in shame and guilt and hide from God. Some are rebellious and won't let God near them. How can God help them when they let their sins separate them from God like this? Does God *want* to punish us? No more than pet owners *want* to punish their pets. As pet owners, we may get angry when the dog chews up our best shoe or when the cat scratches up the couch, but do we stay angry? No, we love our pets and we enjoy petting on them, playing with them, and taking care of them.

What if our pets never got over their guilt of wrongdoing? What if the dog never came out from under the chair? Or, what if the cat never stopped hissing at us every time we tried to pet it? How could we love and take care of our pets if they refused to allow us? Thankfully, our pets get over it pretty quick. Unfortunately, people don't. I know we are not animals, but we often behave the same way with God. We refuse to give the opportunity to God to love us and take care of us. If we want God to hear our prayers and help us, we have to come out from our hiding places and surrender our stubborn and rebellious hearts to him and let him heal us and help us. God wants to answer our prayers, but he can't if we have a wall standing between us and him. We have to tear down that wall and let God in.

Is My Motive Right?

James 4:3, *"You ask and do not receive, because you ask amiss, that you may spend it on your pleasures."*

Sometimes when we are not getting an answered prayer, we should examine ourselves and ask if our motives are right. Why am I asking God for this? Is it for my own selfish desires? Do I want this for the purpose of making myself look better than others? Do I want this answered prayer so that I can use it toward something that is sinful? Will the thing I am asking for eventually hurt someone else? Is it something that goes against God's word?

Further Along, We Will Understand Why In the Sweet By and By

Then, sometimes, we can do our very best for God, have all the faith in the world, and still not get an answered prayer. It is during these times, we just have to resign ourselves to God's will.

If you are a parent, you know that there are times when your child may ask you for something that you know is not good for them. They ask for it because they do not know any better, but you do. So, you as the parent, can not and will not give them specifically what they ask. Out of your love for them, you may give them something else that you know is better for them because you want what is best for them. God is the same with us. What we ask of God sometimes may not be what is best for us even though we don't understand that at the time. God knows what is best for us and wants us to be happy. God gives us what is best for us, but it is up to us to accept this and thank him for it.

Proverbs 20:24 *"A man's steps are of the Lord; How then can a man understand his own way?"*

Jeremiah 10:23 *"O Lord, I know the way of man is not in himself; It is not in man who walks to direct his own steps."*

Chapter Five Study Guide

Part One: Share Your Story

Have you ever prayed for something but did not get an answered prayer, only to realize later that your unanswered prayer was a blessing? Or, can you look back on an unanswered prayer and see that it was for your best?

Part Two: Searching The Scriptures

Can you think of or find any verses from the Bible that relate to prayers not being answered, heard or received by God?

Can you find any examples from the Bible of people who did not receive an answer for their prayers and is there a reason for it?

Part Three: Exercising Your Faith

James 2:26 *"For as the body without the spirit is dead, so faith without works is dead also."*

Exercising our faith by doing good works for God builds our faith, makes us stronger spiritually, and brings us closer to God. Certainly, reading the Bible, praying, lending a helping hand to those in need are good exercises. Consider this as well: Each one of us has a talent or ability. Some of us can teach, some can sing, some can write. Some of us have more education, while others are good cooks or have a talent for a craft or hobby. For each one of us, there is something that we are good at doing.

Think of what you are good at and see how many different ways you can think of to use this talent, ability or knowledge to do good works for God. For example, if you are a good cook, maybe you can cook from time to time for those less fortunate than you, or for someone sick. If you like to write, then write a nice letter or uplifting story for someone who is discouraged. Maybe you like to sing or play music. You could uplift someone who is down with your music. The possibilities are endless. Thinking of them is good exercise in and of itself.

Putting Ourselves To The Test

If we are not getting a response from God, maybe we should take the time to examine ourselves and see if there is anything keeping us from a right relationship with God.

II Corinthians 13:5 *"Examine yourselves as to whether you are in the faith. Test yourselves. Do you not know yourselves, that Jesus Christ is in you unless indeed you are disqualified."*

The apostle Paul here instructs that we should examine ourselves, that we should test our faith. Below is a check list I have created from the chapter. On a scale of 1 to 10, how would you rate yourself? After you complete the checklist, you can look at yourself, see where you need improving and set goals for yourself to grow and improve.

1. I exercise my faith often. (I read the Bible, pray, try to do good for others when I have opportunity, use my talent or abilities for God's use)._____

2. Every day, I pay attention to all the many blessings God gives me daily: food, clothing, job, transportation, health, friends, sunshine, rain, nature's beauty, etc_____

3. I thank God daily for all the blessings he gives me._____

4. If there is a problem between me and another person, I try to make it right with them so that my relationship will be right with God._____

5. When I pray to God for something, I examine my motives to be sure they are right motives._____

6. I have a two-way relationship with God. I pray to him and ask him for the things I need and desire and I in turn listen to what he has to say and I try to do the things he asks of me._____

7. I accept God's will even if I don't understand it._____

Memory Verse: ***Luke 22:42*** *saying, "Father, if it is your will, take this cup away from me; nevertheless not my will, but yours, be done."*

FOR FURTHER STUDY

Some Bible Passages Regarding Unheard And Unanswered Prayers:

II Chronicles 15:2
Job 27:8, 9; 35:12, 13
Psalm 34;15, 16; 66:18
Proverbs 1:28, 29;15:29
Isaiah 1:15, 16; 59:1
Jeremiah 11:11; 14:12
Ezekiel 8:18
Micah 3:4
Zechariah 7:11-13
Matthew 5:23, 24
John 9:31
James 4:3
I Peter 3:7
I John 3:22

Example From Bible Of Someone Not Receiving An Answered Prayer:

II Samuel 11 and 12 (specifically 12:16-18)

The above scriptures are just some that I chose to include in this study for further reading and research. I do not mean to imply that these are the only scriptures in the Bible relating to this particular subject. I am sure there are many other scriptures that one can search and consider.

978-0-595-47182-9
0-595-47182-X

Printed in the United States
94552LV00006B/10-27/A